The Purpose of Parables

By Michael Penny

ISBN: 978-1-78364-517-6

www.obt.org.uk

****

The Open Bible Trust
Fordland Mount, Upper Basildon,
Reading, RG8 8LU, UK.

Introduction

Introduction

This publication can be used either for personal study and meditation, or for a group Bible Study. Each section starts off with a series of questions (Q1, Q2, Q3 etc.) which could be considered and studied privately or discussed in a group. After each set of questions, suggested answers (A1, A2, A3 etc.) are given which can be compared with those of the individual reader or compared with those of the group.

There have been many books which have endeavoured to explain what the parables mean. These have focused mainly on how the disciples would have understood them and, by application, what Christians today may glean from these parables which will be of spiritual value for believers in the twenty-first century.

However, that is only one half of the audience and only one half of the purpose of the parables. Some of those who heard the parables followed Jesus but there were also the Pharisees and others who opposed Christ, as well as those who were indifferent towards Him. What was the purpose of the parables for these people? What effect did the parables have upon them? What did they see in the parables? This is what we shall focus on in this publication.

Background

Background

As the ministry of our Lord Jesus Christ to the Jews of His day progressed, some who had benefitted from His miracles, or witnessed them, did not heed His teaching. He upbraided the cities of Korazin, Bethsaida and Capernaum for not repenting (Matthew 11:20-24).

Opposition arose, and slowly strengthened. The Pharisees chastised Him for His disciples picking corn on the Sabbath day and eating it (Matthew 12:1-7). However, this was **not** against the Law of Moses which allowed food to be picked and eaten on the Sabbath and other holy days, but did not allow it to be harvested (e.g. compare Leviticus 23:33-35 and 23:39-40; they were to do no regular work, but they could take the best fruit from the trees). It was against one of the Pharisaic additions to the Law, the so-called traditions of the elders (Matthew 15:2). Similarly with healing on the Sabbath, which so infuriated the Pharisees that they plotted how they might kill Him (Matthew 12:9-14).

When Jesus healed a demon-possessed man who was both blind and dumb, the crowd were so astonished that they started to ask, "Could this be the Son of David?" That is, was this Jesus of Nazareth the Messiah, the Christ? This was too much for the Pharisees who accused Christ of healing by the power of Beelzebub, the prince of demons (Matthew 12:22-24). A dreadful accusation!

Then, in spite of all the miracles they had seen, and with supreme hypocrisy, the Pharisees and teachers of the Law said to him, "Teacher, we want to see a miraculous sign from you" (Matthew

12:38). Christ ended up calling them a "wicked generation" (Matthew 12:45).

This sets the scene for the opening words of Matthew 13 which states that large crowds gathered around Jesus and "he told them many things in parables" (verses 2-3). This ushers in a new phase of our Lord's ministry. This was the first time He had used parables. But why did He start to use them? And what was their purpose?

Study 1

Questions

Read the well-known *Parable of the Sower* (Matthew 13:1-17).

Q1. What is implied by the expression "he who has ears, let him hear"?

Q2. What was the reaction of the disciples to Christ speaking in parables?

Q3. What was Christ's answer to the disciples' question of Matthew 13:10?

Q4. To whom do the words of verse 12 refer?

Q5. What two groups of people feature in Christ's answer (verse 11)?

Q6. How does a parable achieve the goal Christ sets out in verse 11?

Answers

A1: What is implied by the expression "he who has ears, let him hear"?

This expression is often expanded in Mark and Luke to "let him who has ears to hear, let him hear". Commenting on this expression, Appendix 142 of *The Companion Bible* states:

> This is an important example of the Figure [of speech] *Polyptoton*, the repetition of the same verb in a different inflection, by which great emphasis is put upon the injunction here given.

Norval Geldenhuys, in his *New London Commentary* on the Gospel of Luke, states that this "probably reflects the emphatic Hebrew use of the absolute infinitive" (page 245).

So when our Lord used these expressions He was calling attention to what He had just said as being important. However, I have also noted that these expressions often follow something that may well be hard to understand. See, for example, Matthew 11:15. There the expression follows the issue of whether John the Baptist was, or was not, Elijah.[1]

The Lord used this expression here, in Matthew 13:9 and again in 13:43, after explaining the parable of the Weeds (Tares). It may well be that He was not only emphasising what He had just taught them, but was also indicating that what He had said may be a little hard to understand. Mark 4:33 suggests this. There we read:

---

[1] For a full discussion of this subject see *Elijah and John the Baptist* by Michael Penny, published by The Open Bible Trust.

With many similar parables Jesus spoke the word to them, as much as they could understand.

All this suggests that for some people parables made His teaching a little harder to understand rather than easier, although the mistaken view that parables made Christ's teaching easier is common amongst many Christians.

A2. What was the reaction of the disciples to Christ speaking in parables?

Luke 8:9 states that after Jesus had told this parable "His disciples asked him what this parable meant." To which, Jesus replied "Don't you understand this parable? How then will you understand any parable?" (Mark 4:13).

Thus the initial reaction of the disciples may have been one of confusion for they did not understand what Christ was saying. There may have been some element of uncertainty, or even incredulity, for they then asked him, "*Why* do you speak to the people in parables?" (Matthew 13:10).

Up to now, and by this time Christ was probably more than half way through His ministry, He had never taught in parables. Rather He had taught plainly and clearly. Thus the disciples were perplexed as to why He had changed. And again ... the idea that parables do not make His teaching clearer, but rather veil it, can be seen by the disciples needing explanations.

A3. What was Christ's answer to the disciples' question of Matthew 13:10?

Christ's answer is found in Matthew 13:11-17, before He went on to give the meaning of the parable of the sower. We shall discuss the details of His explanation as we look at the following questions.

A4. To whom do the words of verse 12 refer?

Matthew 13:12 states, "Whoever has will be given more, and he will have an abundance. Whoever does not have, even what he has will be taken from him." Now these words must not be misunderstood or misapplied. Our Lord was not referring to income, wealth or material possessions. He was referring to spiritual knowledge and understanding. This is made clear from the preceding verse which refers to "the knowledge of the secrets of the kingdom of heaven" and in Luke 8:18 our Lord made it even clearer by telling them:

> "Therefore consider carefully how you listen. Whoever has will be given more; whoever does not have, even what he thinks he has will be taken from him "

A5. What two groups of people feature in Christ's answer (verse 11)?

Christ refers to 'you' and to 'them'. The 'you' refers to the disciples, but we would be wrong to limit it to just the twelve. We know that more than twelve formed the faithful following (see Acts 1:21-23). The historic paintings and the Hollywood movies depicting Jesus with just a dozen men everywhere he went may not be correct. It is quite likely that His entourage was somewhat larger.

The 'them' refers to the two groups we mentioned in the opening section. Those who followed for the miracles, but were not interested in His teaching (Matthew 11:11-24), and those who openly opposed Him (e.g. the Pharisees and Teachers of the Law; Matthew 12); i.e., the indifferent and the oppositional. To these groups we could add those mentioned in John 6:26, those who followed Jesus because He fed them, and also the Sadducees, some of the Sanhedrin and the High Priests.

To sum up: the one group – the 'you' – followed Christ, wanted to understand who He was and what He taught. The other groups – the 'them' – were not interested in who Jesus was or what He taught. They were either indifferent or oppositional.

The purpose of the parables was to enhance the spiritual knowledge of the former group, but diminish the spiritual understanding of the latter. Christ said of this second group, the 'them':

> "Though seeing, they do not see;
> Though hearing, they do not hear or understand."
> (Matthew 13:13)

Thus those who were indifferent or oppositional saw something in a parable, but they did not see the true meaning. They heard the words, but did not perceive or understand what Christ was getting at. They were hardening their hearts

> The purpose of the parables was to enhance the spiritual knowledge of those who followed Christ, but diminish the spiritual understanding of those who were indifferent toward Him or who opposed Him.

against both Christ and His teaching, and so He described them in the words of Isaiah 6:9-10, which are then quoted by Matthew:

"You will be ever hearing but never understanding; you will be ever seeing but never perceiving. For this people's heart has become calloused; they hardly hear with their ears, and they have closed their eyes. Otherwise they might see with their eyes, hear with their ears, understand with their hearts and turn, and I would heal them." (Matthew 13:14-15)

This judgmental prophecy from Isaiah is the most quoted Old Testament prophecy[2] in the New Testament. Its final proclamation came at the end of the Acts of the Apostles: see Acts 28:25-27.

A6. How does a parable achieve the goal Christ sets out in verse 11?

A parable contains a spiritual message that the initiated were meant to see, but was couched in words which those who were indifferent or oppositional did not see. It would seem, however, that Christ's followers did not always understand the meaning of a parable

> How did parables hide or conceal the spiritual message from the indifferent and oppositional, and how would these people have reacted to the parables?

(and even with the great benefit of hindsight, neither do we at times) and had to ask Him – a privilege we do not have. However, even though they did not understand the parable, they knew there was something more there, something important, and we will look at the message in some of the more difficult parables later.

---

[2] For a detailed treatment of Isaiah 6 please see *The Most Quoted Old Testament Prophecy* by Michael Penny published by The Open Bible Trust.

For most of this publication, however, the more unusual issue, which is often not dealt with, will be considered; i.e. how did the parables hide or conceal the spiritual message from the indifferent and oppositional, and how would these people have reacted to the parables?

The following, is a précis of a quotation taken from Patrick Fairbairn's *Imperial Bible-dictionary* of 1866.

> The Lord's use of parables was that in them He might accomplish His great work of laying bare the hearts of men, dividing them into two classes – the spiritual and the carnal. As a consequence, He spoke parables so that on the carnal mind, determined to be carnal, He might inflict a deeper blindness, whilst the spiritual, aspiring after greater spirituality, might gain precious wisdom and have the joy of discovering it.

Study 2

Questions

Q7. Look up some definitions of a parable. How would you define a parable?

Q8. Are all parables easy to understand?

Q9. Which of Christ's parables do you find the most difficult to understand?

Q10. What techniques did Christ use to distract indifferent and oppositional people away from the spiritual message in a parable?

Answers

A7. Look up some definitions of a parable. How would you define a parable?

One has often heard that a parable is an earthly story with a heavenly meaning. However, here are some more appropriate definitions.

- *Oxford Illustrated Dictionary*: Fictitious narrative used to point a moral or illustrate some spiritual relation or condition; short allegory.
- *Webster's New World College Dictionary*: A short simple story, usually of an occurrence of a familiar kind, from which a moral or religious lesson may be drawn.
- *Vine's Expository Dictionary of New Testament Words*: lengthy narrative drawn from nature or human circumstances, the object of which is to set forth a spiritual lesson.
- *Strong's Exhaustive Concordance and Dictionary*: comparison, figure, proverb.

There is much sense in all of these definitions, if looked at from the position of those who were sympathetic to Jesus and His teaching. However, none really address the situation from the point of view of the indifferent and oppositional. If a parable was no more that a simple story, how was the spiritual meaning hidden?

The word 'parable' comes from two Greek words: *para*, which means 'near' or 'beside', and *bole*, which means to 'cast' or 'throw'. Thus *parabole* literally signifies one thing 'cast beside' another. Consider 'parallel' lines; that is, one line cast beside another.

Now when we cast one thing beside a second, we can do this either to highlight and make the second clearer, or we can mask the second, and make it less clear. Consider the following sentence.

> In mathematics ▮▮▮▮▮▮▮ is a curve that goes off to infinity.

Here we have cast a box in parallel to part of a sentence, but *in front* of it. This hides part of the sentence and many of us may not be able to make any sense of it. Those with some mathematical expertise would have some suggestions about what could or could not be behind the box. However, if, instead, we cast the box in parallel, but *behind* the words, they become clearer and are emphasised.

> In mathematics **an hyperbola** is a curve that goes off to infinity.

It would seem that by using parables Christ was doing the former. He was, in some way, masking truth for those who were indifferent or oppositional.

A8. Are all parables easy to understand?

Some parables, to us, seem very easy to understand. For example, the Good Samaritan and the Lost Son are two popular ones with clear messages. We are then left wondering, how were the spiritual lessons in such parables as these hidden from the 'them' – that second group of people?

A9. Which of Christ's parables do you find the most difficult to understand?

Probably one of the most perplexing of parables is the one of the Shrewd Manager (Luke 16:1-13). There we read such things as:

- The master commended the dishonest steward.
- The people of this world are shrewder in dealing with their own kind than are the people of the light.
- I tell you, use worldly wealth to gain friends for yourselves, so that when it is gone, they may be welcomed into eternal dwellings.

None of the above statements seem right, from the Christian viewpoint, so what is going on here? (We shall return to this parable later.)

A10. What techniques did Christ use to distract indifferent and oppositional people away from the spiritual message in a parable?

Earlier we made mention of the curve called the hyperbola, a curve which goes off to infinity and looks like this.

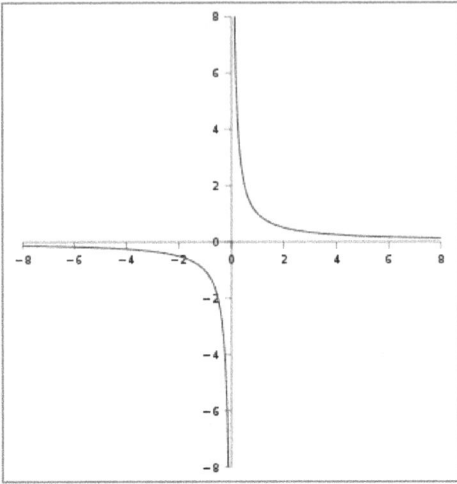

This hyperbola goes off to infinity in all four directions and gives rise to the figure of speech known as hyperbole – an exaggerated statement not meant to be taken literally. However, a *parabola* is a curve which also goes off to infinity, albeit in only two directions.

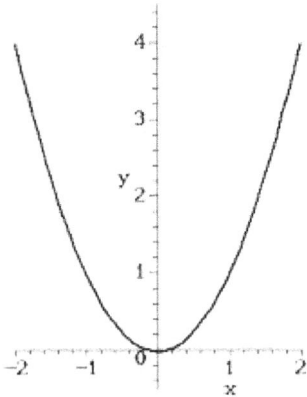

So could it be that a *parable* contains an extreme exaggeration, or something not meant to be taken literally? Something that would cause the ears of the initiated to prick up and want to know more, but would cause the indifferent and oppositional to laugh, or scoff, or deride? We do read that the Pharisees sneered after one of the parables (Luke 16:14).

Study 3

Questions

Q11. Read the parables of the sower (Matthew 13:1-9) and the weeds (Matthew 13:24-30).

What, in each of these two parables, is an exaggeration or something not meant to be taken literally, and which may cause the indifferent or oppositional to laugh, scoff or deride?

Q12. The following are the rest of the parables in Matthew 13. Can you see what is extreme in each one?

   (a) The Mustard Seed (Matthew 13:31-32).
   (b) The Yeast or Leaven (Matthew 13:33).
   (c) The Hidden Treasure (Matthew 13:44).
   (d) The Pearl (Matthew 13:45).
   (e) The Net of Fish (Matthew 13:47-50).

Answers

A11(a). The Parable of the Sower[3] (Matthew 13:1-9).

No doubt those listening to the words of this parable, both the initiated and the indifferent or oppositional, did so with interest. However, as Jesus reached the climax of the story, one can imagine the former group being perplexed and the latter group becoming incredulous – either laughing or scoffing. The problem is verse 9.

> "Still other seed fell on good soil, where it produced a crop - a hundred, sixty or thirty times what was sown."

We today, with our hybrid grains or genetically modified ones, can easily pass over this statement. However, in Israel at that time, with its poor soil and lack of grain, they were lucky to get ten-fold. To talk of thirty fold or sixty fold was bad enough, but a hundred fold! Was that a joke? Those who opposed Jesus could easily have seen it as one or dismissed Him as a man who knew nothing much about farming! That could well have been the attitude of the indifferent and oppositional.

However, the initiated, although pulled up by this verse, may have recalled Isaac who did, because the Lord blessed him, miraculously produce a hundredfold (Genesis 26:12). They, as we have seen, did not understand the parable but were not dismissive and asked the Lord for an explanation.

---

[3] For a full treatment of this passage please see *The Parable of the Sower* by Nico Baalbergen published by The Open Bible Trust.

A11(b). The Parable of the Weeds (Matthew 13:24-30)

There have been a number of explanations which state that the weeds (tares) are indistinguishable from the wheat, and so should not be pulled out. However, that is not the issue. The fact is that any experienced farmer or gardener would soon tell if what is growing is not what he planted. That being the case, he would pull out the foreign plant as soon as possible. That would have been even more the case in the land of Israel in Christ's time. With poor soil and lack of rain, the weeds would take the goodness and moisture away from the wheat. Thus to leave the weeds to grow would have been absurd! Those who opposed Christ could have dismissed Him as a man who knew nothing about plants and one who should stick to carpentry! That could well have been the reaction of the indifferent and oppositional.

However, the initiated could tell there was something more behind this. It didn't seem to make sense but Jesus didn't talk nonsense so they went to Him and asked Him to explain it to them.

A12. The following are the rest of the parables in Matthew 13. Can you see what is extreme in each one?

A12(a) The Mustard Seed (Matthew 13:31-32).

The listeners would have been familiar with the simile of high trees representing world powers (Ezekiel 31; Daniel 4). However, the tiny mustard seed, although it produces a large plant ... it does not become a tree! This, again, would give those who were indifferent or oppositional the opportunity to scoff at Christ and question His knowledge of plants. They would be more intent on watching for something to criticise, than in looking for the spiritual message about the kingdom of heaven.

A12(b) The Yeast or Leaven (Matthew 13:33).

The listeners were familiar with yeast as a symbol of sin (see Exodus 12:15 and also the Feast of Unleavened Bread and the Passover). Christ also warned his disciples, "Be on your guard against the yeast of the Pharisees, which is hypocrisy" (Luke 12:1; see also Matthew 16:6,11; Mark 8:15). A tiny amount of yeast will slowly spread through the whole dough, and so sin will spread and corrupt society.

But Christ unexpectedly introduces this symbol of sin into the kingdom of heaven. This would open Christ to the charge of not understanding the symbolism of the Scriptures. Those who were concerned with deriding Him would miss the point that the kingdom of heaven upon earth will start small but will spread throughout the whole world.

A12(c) The Hidden Treasure (Matthew 13:44).

Here, the man, having found a treasure in someone else's field, hid it from the owner of the field. He then sold all that he owned so that he can buy that field. This is not only dishonest – cheating the owner of the field – but also, by having sold everything he owned, what was the man and his family going to live on? He would have to sell the treasure.

A12(d) The Pearl (Matthew 13:45).

The merchant here was not dishonest, but he had the same dilemma as the man who sold everything to buy the field. If the merchant sold everything he had, what was he going to live on?

A12(e) The Net of Fish (Matthew 13:47-50).

Apparently the two most common fish in Galilee were carp and catfish, but there were others such as damselfish and scaleless bennies. Verse 48 speaks of 'good' fish and 'bad' fish, but *The Living Bible* has:

> When the net is full, he drags it up onto the beach and sits down and sorts out the edible ones into crates and throws the others away. (Matthew 13:48)

The 'good' fish were the edible ones and the 'bad' fish were those which could not be eaten. The latter may have been the unclean fish according to the Law of Moses, and these would be thrown away.

> Of all the creatures living in the water you may eat any that has fins and scales. But anything that does not have fins and scales you may not eat; for you it is unclean. (Deuteronomy 14:9-10; see also Leviticus 11:9-12)

This would mean that fish such as the carp and damselfish would be the clean, 'good' fish, but the catfish and scaleless bennies would be the unclean, 'bad' fish.

At first reading I thought that throwing unclean fish back into the lake of Galilee would have been the absurdity, as these would either breed more unclean fish or, if they were dead, would pollute this small lake. However, on looking more closely, it does not say that. It says they were 'on shore' when the bad fish were thrown away.

However, were the unclean 'bad' fish simply thrown away, or would the fishermen have sold them at a lower price, for example to feed animals? Or to crush them and use them as fertiliser? If it was normal practice at that time to sell the unclean fish, then simply to throw them away would have been illogical.

****

In all of the parables in Matthew 13 we can see that there was something unusual which those opposed to Christ could latch on to and question and query. With their critical attitude this would be the focus of their attention, and distract them from the message that Christ was giving.

Study 4

Questions

Q13. In each of the following four parables, suggest what may be an exaggeration or something not meant to be taken literally, and which may cause the indifferent or oppositional to laugh, scoff or deride?

    (a) The Good Samaritan (Luke 10:25-37).
    (b) The Lost Sheep (Luke 15:1-7).
    (c) The Lost Coin (Luke 15:8-10).
    (d) The Lost Son (Luke 15:11-32).

Q14. Read The Parable of the Unmerciful Servant; (Matthew 18:23-35). What is extreme in this account that would distract the indifferent and oppositional?

Answers

A13(a). The Parable of the Good Samaritan (Luke 10:25-37).

The man, a Jew, was going from Jerusalem to Jericho and fell among robbers. The first person to come along was a priest – and most priests were Sadducees. The second person was a Levite.

Levi was one of the twelve sons of Jacob, and his descendants formed one of the Twelve Tribes of Israel. They became the priestly tribe. Aaron, who was of the tribe of Levi, became the first high priest and Aaron's descendants held a special position in the priesthood as they were the ones who offered sacrifices etc., in the temple in Jerusalem. The Levites were the other members of Levi's tribe who performed the other, lesser, priestly duties.

Having had these two religious people pass by the helpless man, it must have been obvious to those listening that Jesus was going to have a go at the Sadducees and the religious community, and that the hero was going to be someone insignificant in the religious world. A shepherd; a fisherman; a tax collector even ... but no ... a Samaritan! But Jews do not associate with Samaritans (John 4:9), and Samaritans did not welcome Jews (Luke 9:52-53).

The details of the antagonism between Jews and Samaritans are beyond the scope of this publication, but it went back centuries, to when those Jews who returned from Babylon to rebuild Jerusalem and the Temple would not associate with those who returned from the Assyrian captivity. To have a Samaritan helping a Jew ... well that was unbelievable! Some may have wondered whether Jesus was joking. Others may have queried His knowledge of the history of Israel!

One can see that a statement about a Samaritan helping a Jew would take the minds of the indifferent and oppositional away from the spiritual teaching in this parable.

A13(b). The Parable of the Lost Sheep (Luke 15:1-7).

Not only could those opposed to Christ question his knowledge of farming and gardening, and the history of Israel, they could easily come to the conclusion that He knew nothing about being a shepherd. In this parable a shepherd goes off and leaves ninety-nine sheep unattended to look for one! If that happened, when he got back, how many of those ninety-nine would still be around? They would have wandered here, there and everywhere, and how many would have been killed by wolves?

A13(c). The Parable of the Lost Coin (Luke 15:8-10).

The silver coins in question here were drachma. The footnote in the *NIV* suggests that one drachma was about a day's wage. However, can one picture a person who had been careless enough to lose such a coin, then calling all her friends and neighbours together? Maybe ... maybe not! But one can imagine a degree of scepticism in the minds of the indifferent and oppositional. "Really?" would have been a possible reaction.

A13(d). The Parable of the Lost Son. (Luke 15:11-32).

As this story unfolds one can imagine a sense of shock amongst those present, especially the Pharisees (Luke 15:2), when Jesus got to the point that the lost son ...

> ... went and hired himself out to a citizen of that country, who sent him to his fields to feed *pigs*. (Luke 15:15)

And what then followed may have caused some to shudder. They heard ...

> He longed to fill his stomach with the pods that the pigs were eating. (Luke 15:16)

But if that wasn't enough, we read that on the return journey ...

> But while he [the lost son] was a long way off, his father saw him and was filled with compassion for him; he ran to his son, threw his arms around him and kissed him. (Luke 15:20)

Not only was it unthinkable that a Jewish father would go out to any son ... he would surely wait for his son to come to him ... but to go out to such a son as this, and touch him, and throw arms around him and then kiss him! This son was unclean! He had been with pigs! He had eaten the food of pigs! The Pharisees, in particular, were so concerned about being ceremonially clean and one can imagine that their reaction to this parable would easily have blocked its spiritual message.

The attitude of the older son towards his returning brother is also pretty extreme, and some have suggested that this older son represented the Pharisees and their attitude towards the sinners and tax collectors. However, if the father in the parable represented God, it is doubtful if it could be said of the Pharisees that spiritually they were always with God and that everything He had was theirs (verse 31).

A14. Read The Parable of the Unmerciful Servant; (Matthew 18:23-35). What is extreme in this account that would distract the indifferent and oppositional?

In the footnotes of the *NIV* it is suggested that ten thousand talents is worth over a million pounds, whereas the hundred denarii is but a few pounds. In this way the translators attempt to get over the exaggeration. This has much merit, particularly in its simplicity. However, the exaggeration is even more extreme.

One talent was worth 10,000 denarii. Thus 10,000 talents was worth 10,000 x 10,000 = 100,000,000 denarii. Thus the unmerciful servant owed his master 100 million denarii, but was, himself, owed just 100 denarii. Now if a denarius was the pay for one day's work, 100 denarii was a goodly sum. However, to owe someone 100,000,000 denarii was absurd.

In 4 BC the whole of Galilee and Perea paid taxes to the Romans of just 200 talents; i.e. 200 x 10,000 = 2,000,000 denarii. For a private individual, the servant, to have owed 50 times that amount ... that was unbelievable. It would be like me owing someone 50 times more than all the tax revenue raised by Wales and Scotland!

And not only that, if the master had loaned him that amount, what would the master have been worth? Any who opposed Christ would have had much to take their mind off the teaching of forgiveness.

Study 5

Questions

Q15. Read the parable of the Shrewd Manager (Luke 16:1-13).

(a) Where does the parable end? That is, when does the 'manager' stop speaking and Christ's teaching begin? Is it half way through verse 8, or at the end of verses 8? Or is it at the end of verse 9 or the end of verse 12 or the end of verse 13?

(b) What is extreme in this parable?

(c) About how many trees would be required to produce about 800 gallons (3,000 litres) of olive oil? And about how much money would 400 gallons be worth?

(d) About how many acres would be required to produce about 1,000 bushels of wheat? And about how much money would 200 bushels cost?

(e) Why did the master commend the dishonest steward?

(f) Who said, "The people of this world are more shrewd in dealing with their own kind than are the people of the light"? Are these the words of the master in the parable, or is this the actual teaching of Christ? And are the sentiments expressed true?

(g) Again, who said "I tell you, use worldly wealth to gain friends for yourselves, so that when it is gone, you will be welcomed into eternal dwellings"? Are these the words of the manager or the actual teaching of Christ? And is this true?

Answers

A15. Read the parable of the Shrewd Manager (Luke 16:1-13).

A15(a) Where does the parable end? That is, when does the 'manager' stop speaking and Christ's teaching begin? Is it half way through verse 8, or at the end of verse 8? Or is it at the end of verse 9 or the end of verse 12 or the end of verse 13?

This is not an easy question to answer, and is discussed more fully later. However, verse 8 starts off with "The master commended ...." and verse 9 commences with "I tell you ..." The "I" must refer to our Lord and so the parable has certainly ceased by then, if not earlier. This means the difficult words of verse 9 come from the mouth of Jesus.

A15(b) What is extreme in this parable?

There is so much in this parable that is extreme that even the most casual student of the Bible, when reading it, is somewhat perplexed! What is going on here? What is the manager doing? What is the master saying? Little of it makes sense until verse 10 but by then the parable is over and we are back to the clear teaching of Jesus. In fact, where does the parable end? Answering the next questions will make the exaggerations clear.

A15(c) About how many trees would be needed to produce 800 gallons (3,000 litres) of olive oil? And about how much money would 400 gallons cost?

The Greek has one hundred *batous* and some translations have simply "one hundred *measures*". Some versions have 750 gallons, some have 800 and some have 900 – and of course, the American gallon is smaller than the imperial one! However, it is suggested that this volume of oil would require about 150 trees – and assuming this person was not the only purchaser of olive oil from the "rich man" who owned the orchards, it must have been a very big orchard and he must have been a very wealthy man.

It has been suggested that this quantity of olive oil would have cost in the region of 1,000 denarii; thus the manager was giving this customer 500 denarii – and a denarius was, on average, a day's pay.

A15(d) About how many acres would be required to produce about 1,000 bushels of wheat? And about how much money would 200 bushels cost?

The Greek has one hundred *korous* and, again, some translations have "one hundred *measures*". Others have values of between 1,000 and 1,200 bushels (37,000 – 45,000 litres). To produce such a quantity would require about 100 acres and, assuming this person was not the only purchaser of wheat from the "rich man" who owned the fields, he must have owned a very large farm! Today we think nothing of farms of 1,000 or more acres, but in New Testament times this was far from the case. We can see from this answer, and the previous one, this man must have owned an enormous farm and been absurdly rich.

It has been suggested that 1,000 bushels of wheat would cost about 2,500 denarii and so cancelling 200 bushels would mean taking 500 denarii off the bill.

With these two customers alone the shrewd manager gave away 1,000 denarii; getting on for three years' wages. He must have hoped that these people would be so indebted to him and that they would befriend him until he could secure another lucrative position. That being the case, why did the rich owner commend him?

A15(e) Why did the master commend the dishonest steward?

In verse 8 we read, "The master commended the dishonest manager *because* he had acted shrewdly." The *KJV* has, "And the lord commended the unjust steward, *because* he had done wisely."

The word translated "commended" is the Greek *epaineo*, which means to '*greatly* praise', being "an intensive form of *aineo*" (W E Vine). So this is 'over the top' praise. Perhaps we should say that the master was being ironic, even sarcastic. "Brilliant. Well done. You have acted so wisely ... Now let's call the police!" (Not that they had police in those days, but the manager would have been taken to the authorities.)

A15(f) Who said, "The people of this world are more shrewd in dealing with their own kind than are the people of the light"? Are these the words of the master in the parable, or is this the actual teaching of Christ? And are the sentiments expressed true?

Clearly the first half of verse 8 is spoken by the master in the parable. But the second sentence refers to "the people of the light", an expression that fits more with Christ than it does with the master. Christ said of the master:

The master commended the dishonest manager because he had acted *shrewdly.*

Then our Lord picked up on this statement and developed it.

For the people of this world are *more shrewd* in dealing with their own kind than are the people of the light. (Luke 16:8)

The word translated 'shrewdly' in the first part of the verse is the Greek *phronimos* and 'more shrewd' is *phronimoteros*, which, by comparison, shows a greater degree of wisdom or shrewdness. So it would seem, again, that the Lord here was not expressing 'the truth', but was continuing the irony.

Paul, at least twice, uses this word *phronomos* in an ironic or sarcastic way. In the following verses it is translated 'wise'.

We are fools for Christ, but you are so wise in Christ! We are weak, but you are strong! You are honoured, we are dishonoured! (1 Corinthians 4:10)

You gladly put up with fools since you are so wise! (2 Corinthians 11:19)

The *Living Bible* suggests that an ellipsis, an implied word, should be supplied. It has:

And it is true that the citizens of this world are more clever [in dishonesty] than the godly are. (Luke 16:8)

Whether or not this is correct, I do not know, but the sentiments expressed in that translation are indeed true.

A15(g) Again, who said "I tell you, use worldly wealth to gain friends for yourselves, so that when it is gone, you will be welcomed into eternal dwellings"? Are these the words of the manager or the actual teaching of Christ? And is this true?

As this verse opens with "I tell you ..." these are clearly the words of Christ Himself, His actual teaching, and not an expression put into the mouth of the manager. However, what the Lord says here, at face value, is simply not correct.

Having put ironic or sarcastic words in the mouth of the master, and continuing the irony Himself in verse 8, was the Lord here (verse 9) being even more ironic? That is a distinct possibility. However, the words of the *Living Bible* are again interesting.

> But shall I tell you to act that way, to buy friendship through cheating? Will this ensure your entry into an everlasting home in heaven? (Luke 16:9)

Here we have two rhetorical questions, each demanding the answer "No!"

- "No! I do not tell you to act that way, and to buy friendships through cheating!"
- "No! I do not tell you that this will ensure your entry into an everlasting home in heaven!"

And the same sentiments are expressed in the notes of *The Companion Bible*. Here, at Luke 16:9, we read the following:

> And do I say unto you ...? Is this what I say to you ...? In verses 10-12, the Lord gives the reason why He does not

say that; otherwise these verses are wholly inconsequent, instead of being the true application of verses 1-8.

Another possibility is to look upon the words which Christ said in Luke 16:9 and parallel them with what Paul wrote to Timothy.

Luke 16:9	1 Timothy 6:17-19
I tell you, use worldly wealth to gain friends for yourselves, so that when it is gone, you will be welcomed into eternal dwellings.	Command those who are rich in this present world not to be arrogant nor to put their hope in wealth, which is so uncertain, but to put their hope in God, who richly provides us with everything for our enjoyment. Command them to do good, to be rich in good deeds, and to be generous and willing to share. In this way they will lay up treasure for themselves as a firm foundation for the coming age, so that they may take hold of the life that is truly life.

In this case, Christ was telling his disciples that people should use worldly wealth wisely, for the benefit of others and this contrasts with the parable which is about the misuse of another's money, and Christ concludes with the well-known words "You cannot serve both God and money" (verse 13).

What was the reaction of those who heard the words of this parable?

> The Pharisees, who loved money, heard all this and were sneering at Jesus". (Luke 16:14)

The Pharisees, who dearly loved their money, naturally scoffed at all this. (Luke 16:14; *The Living Bible*)

The Pharisees not only loved money and were rich, they were also hypocrites. They taught that the rich would suffer in the next life, but the poor would be blessed, yet they did nothing to divest themselves of their wealth. Their hypocrisy on this subject is shown in the next parable, the Rich Man and Lazarus.

Study 6

Questions

Q16. First read the parable of the Rich Man and Lazarus (Luke 16:19-31) and then read the Appendix on page 61 before answering the questions below.

(a) To whom is this parable addressed?

(b) Read the parable of the Rich Man and Lazarus again. What similarities do you notice between Luke 16:19-31 and Josephus's discourse on *hades*?

(c) What would the people of Jesus' day find as an exaggeration?

Answers

A16. Read the parable of the Rich Man and Lazarus (Luke 16:19-31) and then read Appendix 1 on page 33.

It is often a surprise to many Christians when they find out that the gist of Luke 16:19-31 is not Christ revealing something new, but that He was, in fact, using the Pharisees' own teaching, adding to it, adapting it, and turning it against them.

Appendix 1 is part of the works of Josephus, the first century Jewish historian who wrote mainly for the Romans and also for the Greeks. This is 'An extract out of Josephus' discourse to the Greeks concerning *hades*'.

A16(a) To whom is this parable addressed?

Following on from the parable of the Shrewd Manager (Luke 16:1-13) and Christ's comments after it, we read:

> The Pharisees who loved money heard all this and were sneering at Jesus.

We then read:

> He [Jesus] said to them ...

And the rest of Luke 16, including the parable of the Rich Man and Lazarus, is addressed to the Pharisees.

A16(b) Read the parable of the Rich Man and Lazarus again. What similarities do you notice between Luke 16:19-31 and Josephus's discourse on *hades*?

Josephus' discourse on *hades* provides us with a valuable insight into the teachings of the Pharisees as it records what the Pharisees taught regarding "*hades*", "the intermediate state", "Abraham's bosom", "punishments", etc. So to understand the parable of *The Rich Man and Lazarus*, and its impact upon people like the Pharisees, we need to understand at least some of their views and teaching[4]. Some of the similarities between Luke 16:19-31 and Josephus are as follows:

Hades, see *NIV* footnote on 'hell' in Luke 16:23, is, according to Josephus, a subterraneous region which is the destiny of all, *both good and bad*, and where some people are punished (paragraph 1), and 'torments' are mentioned in Luke 16:23.

Luke 16:22 refers to 'angels' and so does Josephus (paragraph 1). Luke 16:22 also mentions 'Abraham's bosom' (*KJV*) and so does Josephus (paragraph 3). From reading Josephus, however, we find that this is not a part of heaven, as some Christians surmise, but part of *hades*. According to the Pharisees, at death some went to the part known as 'Abraham's bosom', while others went to a different part of *hades*.

Luke 16:24 speaks of 'fire' and so does Josephus (paragraph 2).

Josephus wrote of a "chaos deep and large" fixed between these two regions, and Luke 16:26 has "a great chasm has been fixed". The similarity here is striking.

---

[4] For a full treatment of this parable please see *The Rich Man and Lazarus* by E W Bullinger published by The Open Bible Trust.

Josephus (paragraph 4)	Luke 16:26
for a *chaos* deep and large is fixed between them; insomuch that a just man that hath compassion upon them cannot be admitted, nor can one that is unjust, if he were bold enough to attempt it, pass over it.	And beside all this, between us and you a great chasm has been fixed, so that those who want to go from here to you cannot, nor can anyone cross over from there to us.

Also, in paragraph 6, Josephus states that "the interceding prayers of their kindred" will not profit them, and this is what we find in Luke 16:27-31.

A16(c) The parable of the Rich Man and Lazarus (Luke 16:19-31). What would the people of Jesus' day find as an exaggeration?

As Christ began this parable the ears of the Pharisees, and those familiar with their teaching, would have pricked up. Was Jesus going to endorse *their* teaching? After all, He has started quoting it!

The words from the rich man in verse 24 elicited a response from the fictional Abraham of the parable which was in complete accord with what the Pharisees taught (verses 25-26). Although, to us, there may appear things quite extreme in these verses, there would have been nothing alien or unusual to those who were familiar with the Pharisees and their views.

The second request from the rich man asked Abraham to raise Lazarus from the dead and send him to his father's house, to warn his five brothers, so that they will avoid joining him in torment.

This would mean that the five brothers would have had to divest themselves of their wealth. This would make the Pharisees either a little uncomfortable (for they could construe this as Christ having a go at them and their riches) or bring a wry smile to their face (for although the Pharisees taught this, to keep the poor happy, they did not believe it themselves).

However, Abraham was unsympathetic to this request and simply stated that the brothers should listen to what was written in the Law of Moses and the Prophets. At this the Pharisees may have felt even more uncomfortable and any smiles may have disappeared. The Pharisees were great ones for either adding to the Law of Moses or detracting from it[5], whichever suited them best.

But the rich man did not give up. He argued that the Law and the Prophets would not be as powerful as someone rising from the dead. But the Abraham in this parable firmly denied this by stating:

> "If they do not listen to Moses and the Prophets, they will not be convinced even if someone rises from the dead." (Luke 16:31)

This is the climax of the parable and how would the Pharisees, and those who opposed Christ, have reacted? "A good tale!" "A likely story!" And no doubt they would have said, "Of course we would believe if someone came back from *hades*!"

---

[5] For example, see Matthew 15:1-6 where their traditions added to the Law by making it compulsory to wash before eating, yet they detracted from the Law by allowing people to abrogate their responsibility to their aged parents.

However, this seems to be a prophetic parable. Some think that in verse 31 Jesus was referring to His own resurrection, but this seems unlikely. Although the Lord did not give the rich man a name, he did call the beggar 'Lazarus' and, of course, the Lord did raise someone called Lazarus from the dead ... and what was the reaction of those who opposed Christ to this wonderful miracle?

> Therefore many of the Jews who had come to visit Mary, and had seen what Jesus did [in raising Lazarus], put their faith in him. But some of them went to the Pharisees and told them what Jesus had done. Then the chief priests and the Pharisees called a meeting of the Sanhedrin. "What are we accomplishing?" they asked. "Here is this man performing many miraculous signs. If we let him go on like this, everyone will believe in him, and then the Romans will come and take away both our place and our nation." Then one of them, named Caiaphas, who was high priest that year, spoke up, "You know nothing at all! You do not realize that it is better for you that one man die for the people than that the whole nation perish." He did not say this on his own, but as high priest that year he prophesied that Jesus would die for the Jewish nation, and not only for that nation but also for the scattered children of God, to bring them together and make them one. So from that day on they plotted to take his life. (John 11:45-53)

And not only did they plan to kill Christ, they also wanted to do away with the evidence by killing Lazarus.

> Meanwhile a large crowd of Jews found out that Jesus was there and came, not only because of him but also to see

Lazarus, whom he had raised from the dead. So the chief priests made plans to kill Lazarus as well, for on account of him many of the Jews were going over to Jesus and putting their faith in him. (John 12:9-11)

Thus the words which ended the parable were indeed true. These people did not listen to Moses and the Prophets, and neither were they convinced when Lazarus rose from the dead.

****

But what about that greater resurrection? What effect did the Lord Jesus rising from the dead have on them?

Strong opposition from the High Priests, the Sanhedrin and many other Jewish leaders continued throughout the Acts of the Apostles and we see the Apostles imprisoned, beaten, stoned. However, surprisingly and pleasingly, some of the Pharisees did become believers (Acts 15:5) and so did a large number of the priests, who were mostly Sadducees (Acts 6:7).

The resurrection of Christ Himself is not the climax of the parable of the Rich Man and Lazarus, for, as we have just seen, after He was raised some of the indifferent and oppositional Pharisees and Sadducees did finally believe. Thanks be to God.

Appendix

Appendix

Josephus's discourse to the Greeks concerning *hades* records what the Pharisees taught regarding the "intermediate state", "Abraham's bosom", etc.. It is a valuable insight into their teaching and is reproduced here, without comment. We trust that the reader may gain a fuller picture of how far their teachings strayed from what was taught in the Scriptures and how some modern-day views have more in common with this extract than they do with the New Testament.

An extract from Josephus's Discourse to the Greeks concerning Hades

1) Now as to, wherein the souls of the righteous and unrighteous are detained, it is necessary to speak of it. Hades is a place in the world not regularly finished; a *subterraneous* region, wherein the light of this world does not shine, from which circumstance, that in this region the light does not shine, it cannot be but there must be in it perpetual *darkness*. This region is allotted as a place of custody for souls, in which angels are appointed as guardians to them, who distribute to them *temporary punishments*, agreeable to every one's behaviour and manners.

2) In this region there is a certain place set apart, as *a lake of unquenchable fire*, whereinto we suppose no one hath hitherto been cast; but it is prepared for a day afore determined by God, in which one righteous sentence shall deservedly be passed upon all men; when the unjust and those that have been disobedient to God, and have given honour to such idols as have been the vain

operations of the hands of men, as to God himself, shall be adjudged to this *everlasting punishment*, as having been the causes of defilement; while the just shall obtain *an incorruptible* and never-fading *kingdom*. These are now indeed confined in Hades, but not in the same place wherein the unjust are confined.

3) For there is one descent into this region, at whose gate we believe there stands an archangel with an host; which gate when those pass through that are conducted down by the angels appointed over souls, they do not go the same way; but the just are guided to the *right hand*, and are led with hymns, sung by the angels appointed over that place, unto a region of *light*, in which the just have dwelt from the beginning of the world; not constrained by necessity, but ever enjoying the prospect of the good things they see, and rejoice in the expectation of those new enjoyments which will be peculiar to every one of them, and esteeming those things beyond what we have here; with whom there is no place of toil, no burning heat, no piercing cold, nor are any briers there; but the countenance of the *fathers* and of the just, which they see always smiles upon them, while they wait for that rest and eternal new *life in heaven*, which is to succeed this region. This place we call *The Bosom of Abraham*.

4) But as to the unjust, they are dragged by force to the *left hand* by the angels allotted for punishment, no longer going with a good-will, but as prisoners driven by violence; to whom are sent the angels appointed over them to reproach them and threaten them with their terrible looks, and to thrust them still downwards. Now those angels that are set over these souls, drag them into the neighbourhood of hell itself; who, when they are hard by it, continually hear the noise of it, and do not stand clear of the hot vapour itself; but when they have a nearer view of this spectacle, as of a terrible and exceeding great prospect of fire, they are

struck with a fearful expectation of a future judgement, and in effect punished thereby; and not only so, but where they see the place (or choir) of the *fathers* and of the just, even hereby are they punished; for a *chaos* deep and large is fixed between them; insomuch that a just man that hath compassion upon them cannot be admitted, nor can one that is unjust, if he were bold enough to attempt it, pass over it.

5) This is the discourse concerning Hades, wherein the souls of all men are confined until a proper season, which God hath determined, when he will make a resurrection of all men from the dead, not procuring a transmigration of souls from one body to another, but raising again those very bodies, which you Greeks, seeing to be dissolved, do not believe (their resurrection): but learn not to disbelieve it; for while you believe that the soul is created, and yet is made immortal by God, according to the doctrine of Plato, and this in time, be not incredulous; but believe that God is able, when he hath raised to life that body which was made as a compound of the same elements, to make it immortal; for it must never be said of God, that he is able to do some things and unable to do others. We have therefore believed that the body will be raised again; for although it be dissolved, it is not perished; for the earth receives its remains, and preserves them; and while they are like seed, and are mixed among the more fruitful soil, they flourish, and what is sown is indeed sown *bare grain*; but at the mighty sound of God the Creator, it will sprout up, and be raised in a *clothed* and *glorious* condition, though not before it has been dissolved and mixed (with the earth). So that we have not rashly believed the resurrection of the body; for although it be dissolved for a time on account of the original transgression, it exists still, and is cast into the earth as into a potter's furnace, in order to be formed again, not in order to rise again such as it was before, but in a state of purity, and so as

never to be destroyed anymore; and to every body shall its own soul be restored; and when it hath ***clothed itself*** with that body, it will not be subject to misery, but, being itself pure, it will continue with its pure body, and rejoice with it, with which it having walked righteously now in this world, and never having had it as a snare, it will receive it again with great gladness: but as for the unjust, they will receive their bodies not changed, not freed from diseases or distempers, nor made glorious, but with the same diseases wherein they died; and such as they were in their unbelief, the same shall they be when they shall be faithfully judged.

6) For all men, the just as well as the unjust, shall be brought before *God the word*; for to him hath *the Father committed all judgment*; and he, in order to fulfil the will of his Father, shall come as judge, whom we call *Christ.* For Minos and Rhadamanthus are not the judges, as you Greeks do suppose, but he *whom God even the Father hath glorified*; CONCERNING WHOM WE HAVE ELSEWHERE GIVEN A MORE PARTICULAR ACCOUNT, FOR THE SAKE OF THOSE WHO SEEK AFTER TRUTH. This person, exercising the righteous judgment of the Father towards all men, hath prepared a just sentence for every one, according to his works; at whose judgment seat when all men, and angels, and demons shall stand, they will send forth one voice, and say, **JUST IS THY JUDGMENT**; the rejoinder to which will bring a just sentence upon both parties, by giving justly to those that have done well an *everlasting fruition*; but allotting to the lovers of wicked words *eternal punishment*. To these belong the *unquenchable fire*, and that without end, and a certain fiery *worm never dying*, and not destroying the body, but continuing its eruption out of the body with never-ceasing grief; neither will sleep give ease to these men, nor will the night afford them comfort; death will not free

them from their punishment, nor will the interceding prayers of their kindred profit them; for the just are no longer seen by them, nor are they thought worthy of remembrance; but the just shall remember only their righteous actions, whereby they have attained *the heavenly kingdom*, in which there is no sleep, no sorrow, no corruption, no care, no night, no day measured by time, no sun driven in his course along the circle of heaven by necessity, and measuring out the bounds and conversions of the seasons, for the better illumination of the life of men; no moon decreasing and increasing, or introducing a variety of seasons, nor will she then moisten the earth; no burning sun, no Bear turning round (the pole), no Orion to rise, no wandering of innumerable stars. The earth will not then be difficult to be passed over, nor will it be hard to find out the court of Paradise, nor will there be any fearful roaring of the sea, forbidding the passengers to walk on it; even that will be made easily passable to the just, though it will not be void of moisture. Heaven will not then be uninhabitable by men: and it will not be impossible to discover the way of ascending thither. The earth will not be uncultivated, nor require too much labour of men, but will bring forth its fruits of its own accord, and will be well adorned with them. There will be no more generations of wild beasts, nor will the substance of the rest of the animals shoot out any more; for it will not produce men, but the number of the righteous will continue, and never fail, together with righteous angels, and spirits (of God), and with his word, as a choir of righteous men and women that never grow old, and continue in an incorruptible state, singing hymns to God, who hath advanced them to that happiness, by the means of a regular institution of life; with whom the whole creation also will lift up a perpetual hymn from *corruption to incorruption*, as glorified by a splendid and pure spirit. It will not then be restrained by a bond of necessity, but with a lively freedom shall offer up a voluntary hymn, and shall praise him that made them, together with the angels, and spirits, and men now freed *from all bondage.*

7) And now, if you Gentiles will be persuaded by these motives, and leave your vain imaginations about your pedigrees, and gaining of riches and philosophy, and will not spend your time about subtleties or words, and thereby lead your minds into error, and if you will apply your ears to the hearing of the inspired prophets, the interpreters, both of God and of his word, and will believe in God, you shall both be partakers of these things, and obtain the good things that are to come; you shall see the ascent into the immense heaven plainly, and that kingdom which is there; for what God hath now concealed in silence [will be then made manifest], *what neither eye hath seen, nor ear hath heard, nor hath it entered into the heart of men, the things that God hath prepared for them that love him.*

8) *In whatsoever ways I shall find you, in them shall I judge you entirely*; so cries the END of all things. And he who hath at first lived a virtuous life, but towards the latter end falls into vice, these labours by him before endured, shall be altogether vain and unprofitable, even as in a play, brought to an ill catastrophe. Whosoever shall have lived wickedly and luxuriously may repent; however, there will be need of much time to conquer an evil habit, and even after repentance his whole life must be guarded with great care and diligence, after the manner of a body, which, after it hath been a long time afflicted with a distemper, requires a stricter diet and method of living; for though it may be possible, perhaps, to break off the chain of our irregular affections at once, - yet our amendment cannot be secured without the grace of God, the prayers of good men, the help of the brethren, and our own sincere repentance and constant care. It is a good thing not to sin at all; it is also good, having sinned, to repent, - as it is best to

have health always; but it is a good thing to recover from a distemper. *To God be glory and dominion for ever and ever. Amen.*

Other "Question / Answer" publications.
Ideal for personal study or group discussion.

Count your blessings (Ephesians)
Graham Thomason
Ephesians tells us we are 'blessed with every spiritual blessing'.
The first section encourages an open discussion on blessings; the
second section has questions on specific blessings; while the third
section lists and explains the blessings mentioned in Ephesians.

Imitating Christ
W M Henry
Seven studies, with readings and   questions, based on various
passages from the New Testament encouraging the Christian to be
like Christ.

Love in the Bible
Michael Penny
Part 1 has 8 studies on 'love' involving questions and activities.
Part 2 provides answers and other relevant information.

Studies in Jude
Michael Penny
Jude has just 25 verses and this booklet presents some searching
questions for meditation or discussion before presenting
suggested answers.

The Place of Prayer in an Age of Grace
 Michael Penny
Part 1 has over 80 questions for discussion or meditation on the

prayers in Paul's later letters, with suggested answers, for consideration, given in part 2.

That you may know ... (studies in 1 John)
W M Henry

Part 1 contains 8 studies from 1 John, followed by questions for discussion or meditation. Part 2 has comments and suggested answers.

Following Philippians
William Henry and Michael Penny

Each chapter of Philippians is split in two.. The first treatment of each section gives the historical interpretation and is followed by a group of questions, and the second treatment applies the passage to the 21st Century, and this is followed by another group of questions.

Introducing God's Plan
Sylvia and Michael Penny

An overview of God's plan for mankind given in sixteen chapters. After each chapter there are questions and activities.

Manual on the Gospel of John
Michael Penny

Part 1 has over 250 questions on John's Gospel, together with hints for the answers. Part two gives the answers, and part 3 discusses the main themes of the Gospel.

The Balanced Christian Life (Ephesians)
Michael Penny

A series of five studies based on Ephesians exploring the blessing Christians have in Christ and the practical   Christian life which should follow. One page has questions and activities and the facing page has answers, comments and explanations. Ideal for Lent studies but can be used at any time of year.

Further details of the books on these pages
can be seen on

www.obt.org.uk

The books are available from that website and from

The Open Bible Trust
Fordland Mount, Upper Basildon,
Reading, RG8 8LU, UK.

They are also available as eBooks from Amazon and
Apple and as
KDP paperback from Amazon

About the author

Michael Penny was born in Ebbw Vale, Gwent, Wales in 1943. He read Mathematics at the University of Reading, before teaching for twelve years and becoming the Director of Mathematics and Business Studies at Queen Mary's College Basingstoke in Hampshire, England. In 1978 he entered Christian publishing, and in 1984 became the administrator of The Open Bible Trust.

He held this position for seven years, before moving to the USA and becoming pastor of Grace Church in New Berlin, Wisconsin. He returned to Britain in 1999, and is at present the Administrator and Editor of The Open Bible Trust. From 2010 he has been Chairman of Churches Together in Reading, where he speaks in a number of churches of different denominations. He is also a member of the Advisory Committee to Reading University Christian Union and a chaplain at Reading College.

He is lead chaplain for Activate Learning and has set up chaplaincy teams in a number of their colleges including Reading College, The City of Oxford College, Bracknell and Wokingham College, and Blackbird Leys College.

He lives near Reading with his wife and has appeared on Premier Radio and BBC Radio Berkshire many times. He has made several speaking tours of America, Canada, Australia, New Zealand and the Netherlands, as well as others to South Africa and the Philippines. Some of his writings have been translated into German and Russian.

Also by Michael Penny

He has written many books including:

40 Problem Passages,
Galatians: Interpretation and Application,
Joel's Prophecy: Past and Future,
Approaching the Bible,
The Miracles of the Apostles,
The Manual on the Gospel of John
The Bible! Myth or Message?

Plus two written with W M Henry:

The Will of God: Past and Present
Following Philippians.

His latest three books are:

James: His life and letter
Peter: His life and letters.
Paul: A Missionary of Genius

Further details of all these books can be seen on

www.obt.org.uk

from where they can also be ordered.

They are also available as eBooks from Amazon and Apple and
as KDP paperbacks from Amazon.

About this book

The Purpose of Parables

So why did Christ start teaching in Parables? He had not done so for the first part of his ministry ... so why did He start? That is what the disciples wanted to know and His answer was ...

> "Because the knowledge of the secrets of the kingdom of heaven has been given to you, but not to them."

- So who were the 'you' and who were the 'them'?
- And how do parables reveal secrets to the 'you' but conceal the meaning from the 'them'?

www.ingramcontent.com/pod-product-compliance
Lightning Source LLC
Chambersburg PA
CBHW060659030426
42337CB00017B/2696